AMERICAN DEMOCRACY IN ACTION

The Role of President

Cathleen Small

LUCENT
PRESS

Published in 2019 by
Lucent Press, an Imprint of Greenhaven Publishing, LLC
353 3rd Avenue
Suite 255
New York, NY 10010

Produced for Lucent by Calcium Creative Ltd
Designers: Clare Webber and Simon Borrough
Picture researcher: Rachel Blount
Editors: Sarah Eason and Jennifer Sanderson

Picture credits: Cover: Shutterstock: Amadeustx: top; Lee Nanjoo: bottom; Inside:
Shutterstock: Pamela Au: p. 11; Heidi Besen: p. 24; Brandon Bourdages: p. 35b; Orhan Cam:
p. 27; Rob Crandall: pp. 23, 35t; Danielfela: p. 9; Designer491: p. 29; Dnetromphotos: p. 15;
Everett Collection: p. 10; Everett Historical: pp. 30, 31, 38; Nicole S Glass: p. 20; Jstone: pp.
7, 16; A Katz: p. 17; Jeramey Lende: p. 43; Brad McPherson: p. 25; Gregory Reed: p. 13; Mark
Reinstein: p. 12; Ruskpp: p. 19; Rena Schild: pp. 18, 36; Joseph Sohm: pp. 5, 42, 44–45; Txking:
p. 14; Leonard Zhukovsky: p. 33; Wikimedia Commons: Victor Hugo King: p. 40; Marion S.
Trikosko or Thomas J. O'Halloran, photographer: p. 41; U.S. Mission Photo: Eric Bridiers: p. 37.

Cataloging-in-Publication Data

Names: Small, Cathleen.
Title: The role of president / Cathleen Small.
Description: New York : Lucent Press, 2019. | Series: American democracy in action |
Includes glossary and index.
Identifiers: ISBN 9781534564114 (pbk.) | ISBN 9781534564091 (library bound)
Subjects: LCSH: Presidents--United States--Juvenile literature.
Classification: LCC JK517.S63 2019 | DDC 352.230973--dc23

Printed in the United States of America

CPSIA compliance information: Batch #BS18KL: For further information,
contact Greenhaven Publishing, LLC, New York, New York, at 1-844-317-7404.

Please visit our website, www.greenhavenpublishing.com.
For a free color catalog of all our high-quality books,
call toll free 1-844-317-7404 or fax 1-844-317-7405.

Contents

CHAPTER 1

The U.S. Presidency

The president of the United States is sometimes referred to as "the leader of the free world." In some ways, that designation is true. However, "president" is a title of prestige and dignity more than it is of power. The president does have a number of important powers. But, in many ways, they are a symbolic **figurehead** for the nation.

How the Presidency Came to Be

When the **Framers of the Constitution** drafted the document in 1787, they wrote into Article II, Section 1, "The executive Power shall be vested in a President of the United States of America. He shall hold his Office during the Term of four Years, and, together with the Vice President, chosen for the same Term, be elected, as follows." The Constitution goes on to describe how the **electoral college** will be composed and how it will vote for the president and vice president. Most votes in the United States are direct votes, in which the **popular vote** determines the winner. The presidential election is an exception: it is an **indirect vote** by electoral college.

The Presidential Oath

Every president of the United States, starting with George Washington, has recited the same oath of office: "I do solemnly swear (or affirm) that I will faithfully execute the Office of the President of the United States, and will to the best of my Ability, preserve, protect, and defend the Constitution of the United States."

Bill Clinton took the Oath of Office with his wife Hillary by his side in January 1993.

These words are vague in that they do not actually define what a president should or should not do to "preserve, protect, and defend the Constitution."

This has meant that some presidents have found themselves accused of violating the oath. Among them are President Donald Trump, (who some say violated his oath by disclosing classified information to Russia) and three presidents who have been considered for impeachment: Andrew Johnson, Richard Nixon, and Bill Clinton. Impeachment is a charge of misconduct against a person who holds a high public office. Of these three, Johnson and Clinton were found not guilty at their hearings and Nixon resigned before he could actually be impeached.

How the Presidency Has Changed

The Framers were careful to ensure that a president was not given blanket power. Instead, they favored a separation of powers in which power over the nation was divided between three branches of government: the executive branch (which held the president), the legislative branch (which was made up of the two chambers of Congress—the Senate and the House of Representatives), and the judicial branch (which is made up of the Supreme Court and federal courts). The Framers wrote the Constitution so that the president had some power, but was mostly a figurehead. However, presidential power has expanded significantly over the centuries since the Constitution was **ratified**. One such expansion in power has been in the use of executive orders.

Executive Orders

The process by which laws are passed in the United States can take months or years. At times, a president will want to take faster action on something. One way to do so is to use an executive order.

Executive orders allow the president to officially state how the federal agencies beneath them should use their resources. It is not the same as passing a law because the courts of the United States do not necessarily have to uphold the president's wishes on an executive order. In most cases, though, they will do so. However, in rare cases, they will refuse. Recently, a judge in a district court refused to uphold an executive order signed by President Donald Trump to ban immigrants from seven predominantly Muslim countries from entering the United States.

Executing Executive Orders

The executive order takes into account the laws that have already been established in the Constitution and by Congress, and it dictates how resources should be used within those laws. One of the most famous examples of an executive order is the Emancipation Proclamation, issued by President Abraham Lincoln. The order granted freedom to more than three million slaves.

More recently, within a week of taking office, President Donald Trump issued numerous executive orders. One was an order directing the Department of Homeland Security (DHS) to start building a border wall between the United States and Mexico. The order made this a federal priority, and ordered DHS to use already existing funds to begin constructing the wall. No new laws were passed, and no new funding was needed—it was simply an order by the president to begin construction of the wall immediately.

DONALD TRUMP AND EXECUTIVE ORDERS

Nearly all presidents pass executive orders upon entering office. However, President Trump raised eyebrows with his executive orders. In President Obama's first ten days in office in 2009, he signed nine executive orders. In President Trump's first week in office, he signed only six.

Trump's executive orders have raised eyebrows because they concern controversial issues. The border wall with Mexico was a hot topic during his 2016 presidential campaign. He also signed an order to advance the highly contested Dakota Access and Keystone XL pipelines through tribal lands. One of his orders sought to deny federal funding to sanctuary cities, where local officials tend to protect undocumented immigrants from deportation to the best of their ability. That same order also allowed for a weekly updated list of crimes committed by undocumented immigrants to be posted in sanctuary cities. Another order sought to suspend entry of all persons from seven predominantly Muslim countries for 90 days, and suspend entry into the U.S. refugee program for 120 days.

Like other presidents, Trump issued several executive orders when he took office.

CHAPTER 2
Electing the President

The president of the United States is an elected position. In the most basic sense, the citizens of the United States determine who the president will be. However, the actual process of electing the president is a lot more complicated.

Eligibility Requirements

Not just any person can become president of the United States. A person must meet certain eligibility requirements to do so. According to Article II, Section 1, of the U.S. Constitution, "No Person except a natural born Citizen, or a Citizen of the United States, at the time of the Adoption of this Constitution, shall be eligible to the Office of the President; neither shall any Person be eligible to that Office who shall not have attained to the Age of thirty five Years, and been fourteen Years a Resident within the United States." In other words, to be eligible for the office of the president, a person must:

- Be a natural-born citizen of the United States

- Be at least 35 years old

- Have been a United States resident for at least 14 years

When determining eligibility for the president and members of Congress, the Framers of the Constitution debated whether to use "inhabitant" or "resident." They ultimately decided on "resident" because it suggests someone who has been physically present in the United States the entire time.

Some argued that the term "inhabitant" could allow a person to have an address in the United States but live outside of the country.

Originally, the residency part of this particular clause of the Constitution included "in the whole fourteen Years a Resident." This would have allowed potential presidents to establish their residency cumulatively. In other words, a president would have to have been a resident for a total of at least 14 years, but those years did not necessarily have to be in one chunk. However, the Framers ultimately struck the phrase "in the whole," leaving a little more flexibility for potential presidents who may have, for example, lived abroad while serving in the United States military.

Article II, Section 1, clearly states that the president must be a natural-born citizen of the United States. Other high offices in the government can be filled by foreign-born, **naturalized** citizens of the United States, but not the office of president. The Framers of the Constitution felt strongly that the president needed to be a person with undivided loyalty to the United States, and a foreign-born U.S. citizen might hold onto loyalty to their country of origin.

Election Day in a presidential election year is a momentous event in the United States.

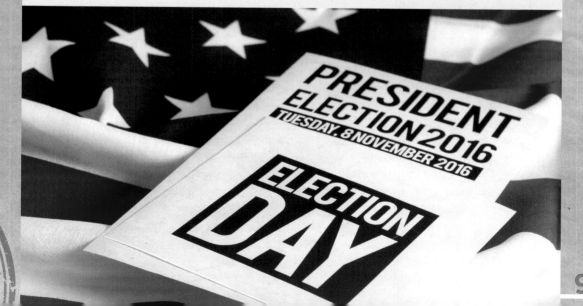

Natural-Born Citizens

One difficulty with the eligibility requirements laid out in the Constitution is the fact that "natural born" is not explicitly defined in the document. It has been interpreted that someone born on U.S. soil is automatically a natural-born citizen, based on a principle in English law known as *jus soli*. However, there is another principle in English law called *jus sanguinis*, which essentially means that citizenship may be passed through blood relation. Following this principle, if parents who are U.S. citizens give birth to a child outside of the United States, that child would automatically receive U.S. citizenship from their parents. The Constitution has not been amended to explicitly support *jus sanguinis*, but the Supreme Court has ruled in favor of it. As a result of that, George Romney, Governor of Michigan, was able to run for president in 1968, even though he had been born outside of the United States.

Citizenship was an issue during Barack Obama's presidency. Some people who did not support Obama's candidacy argued that he was not a natural-born U.S. citizen. Obama's father was Kenyan and his mother was a U.S. citizen. However, when Obama was born in 1961, the law stated that if only one parent was a U.S. citizen at the time of a baby's birth, for the baby to have U.S. citizenship, that parent must have been a U.S. citizen for at least 10 years, at least 5 of which had to be after the age of 16. As Obama's mother was only 18 when he was born, people argued that Obama was not a natural-born U.S. citizen.

Ultimately, Barack Obama produced the birth certificate proving he is indeed a natural-born U.S. citizen.

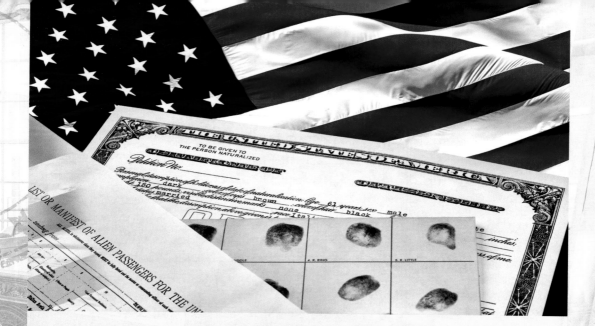

If a person is not a natural-born U.S. citizen, they cannot become president.

The missing information is that the law was written in reference to babies born outside of the United States. Obama was born in Hawaii, two years after Hawaii officially became a state, so the argument against his citizenship is invalid. According to the Fourteenth Amendment, passed in 1868, "All persons born or naturalized in the United States, and subject to the jurisdiction thereof, are citizens of the United States." In other words, even if both of Obama's parents had been foreign citizens, Obama would still be a natural-born U.S. citizen, simply because he was born in Hawaii after it became a state.

Obama is not the only recent presidential candidate to have his citizenship called into question, although it is likely his citizenship received the most attention in the press. John McCain, who ran for president against Obama in 2008, was born in the Panama Canal Zone, which is an unincorporated territory, not an official state. In 1964, presidential nominee Barry Goldwater's citizenship was called into question because he was born in Arizona before it became a state.

The U.S. Electoral System

Once a person has been determined eligible to run for president, they can take part in the U.S. electoral system. Technically, anyone who meets the requirements can run for president. However, the complex electoral system is designed in an attempt to weed out unfit candidates and narrow the field of candidates to those most suitable for the office. Whether this system actually works as intended is a matter of opinion. Some would argue that wholly unfit candidates have become president over the years.

Most serious candidates for president have spent years in the U.S. political system, so they are well known to most citizens—at least in their home state, if not nationally. Some come from a political dynasty, such as John F. Kennedy. His family had been in politics for years and is still heavily involved in politics. Others are well known in their own state. For example, Bill Clinton was governor of Arkansas for years before he became a nationally

known figure when he launched his presidential campaign. A few are known more for being celebrities than anything else. Ronald Reagan was probably best known as a former actor, although he had also served as governor of California. Current president Donald Trump is an exception to the rule: he did not come from a political background, though he is a nationally known figure because of his business enterprise and his work as a television personality.

President Donald Trump does not have a political pedigree. He comes from a business background.

When candidates decide to run for president, they often start preparing years in advance. Campaigns are expensive, and candidates must network and make their name known to raise funds and to test whether citizens are likely to vote for them. If not, a presidential run may not be worth the effort.

Primaries and Caucuses

When a candidate has received contributions or spent more than $5,000 on their campaign, they must register with the Federal Election Committee and file a Statement of Candidacy.

After much campaigning, fundraising, and networking, it becomes time for the primaries and **caucuses**. Primaries are the early elections held by each party in each state to determine who will become the party's nominee for president. Generally, citizens can vote in the primary only for the political party for which they are a registered voter. For example, a citizen registered as a Democrat can vote only in the Democratic primary.

Caucuses are a little different. At a caucus, voters choose delegates to represent them at the national party convention (the Democratic and Republican national conventions are the two most common, though smaller political parties may have conventions, too). In its simplest form, delegates state which candidates they support, then citizens choose the delegates that support their preferred candidate. This is an indirect voting system, rather than the direct voting system used in a primary.

Congresswoman Maxine Waters is a Democrat who represents a district of California.

For the 2016 election, the Republican Party had 17 potential candidates at the beginning of the primaries and caucuses. By the end, it was down to only three. Ultimately, Donald Trump clinched the Republican nomination. The Democratic Party had six potential candidates at the beginning of the primaries. In the end, Hillary Clinton won their nomination.

President Donald Trump used Twitter extensively during his campaign.

The General Election

After the candidates have been formally chosen at the party conventions, it is time for the general election. Campaigning for the general election is intense and often ugly. For years, mudslinging has been a problem, with one party attempting to hurt the chances of the other party by spreading negative information about the other party's candidate. In recent elections, this has become even worse. With the rise of the Internet and social media, people now have a much wider forum for sharing their views. Unfortunately, it is a forum where facts are not necessarily checked, so untrue stories can be spread. For example, all it took was one post about Obama's supposed foreign citizenship for the "news" to spread, creating much doubt about his citizenship and his loyalty to the United States.

The Winning Electoral Votes

■ Republican   ■ Democrat

This map shows how the electoral votes were distributed in the 2016 presidential election.

By the time the general election rolls around in November, citizens have heard plenty about both candidates. Citizens can, in theory, make an informed decision about which candidate will best serve the country. In an election year, on the Tuesday after the first Monday in November, voters head to the polls and cast their votes for president.

The general election is technically an indirect election, although not all citizens are aware of that. When a voter casts a ballot for a presidential candidate, the voter is actually casting a vote for the member of the electoral college who represents their territory. If the majority of voters in a particular territory vote for the Democratic Party, then the elector for that territory will cast an official electoral vote for the Democratic presidential nominee. If the majority of voters in the territory vote Republican, then the elector casts an electoral vote for the Republican candidate. In this way, the member of the electoral college represents the wishes of the majority of citizens in that particular territory.

WHEN THE ELECTORAL COLLEGE BREAKS DOWN

The electoral college system generally works well, although there can be an issue of faithless electors. Faithless electors cast an electoral vote that does not represent the wishes of the majority in their territory. This does not happen very often, but it does happen. For example, in the 2016 election, there were seven faithless electors.

Hillary Clinton won the popular vote by a significant margin—but still lost the electoral vote.

Also, when a candidate wins the presidency because they win the electoral college, yet have lost the popular vote, it can become a source of frustration. Such was the case in the 2016 presidential election, in which Democratic nominee Hillary Clinton won the popular vote by more than 3 million votes—but lost the election because Donald Trump won the electoral college vote. This has happened five times in U.S. history. Presidents John Quincy Adams, Rutherford B. Hayes, Benjamin Harrison, George W. Bush, and Donald Trump have all won the presidency despite losing the popular vote.

Term of Service

Once a president wins the general election, they officially begin their term after the inauguration in the January following the election. Presidents can serve for a maximum of two terms, as set forth in the Twenty-Second Amendment to the Constitution, ratified in 1951. Specifically, Section 1 of the Amendment states, "No person shall be elected to the office of the President more than twice, and no person who has held the office of President, or acted as President, for more than two years of a term to which some other person was elected President shall be elected to the office of President more than once."

This means that if a vice president (or other person) assumes the office of president partway through their predecessor's term, they can run for president one more time—but not twice. That is, unless their assumed term was less than two years, in which case they can run for two more terms. For example, Lyndon B. Johnson took the office of president upon John F. Kennedy's assassination, then ran for a second term.

Before the Twenty-Second Amendment was ratified, one president did serve more than two terms: Franklin Delano Roosevelt. He is the only president to have done so.

HOW WELL DO YOU UNDERSTAND AMERICAN DEMOCRACY?

Particularly since the 2016 election, there has been a movement to abolish, or get rid of, the electoral college and change the presidency to an election by popular vote. What potential problems do you think might arise from this change? What do you think the benefits would be?

The discrepancy between the popular and electoral votes in the 2016 election stirred up much controversy.

CHAPTER 3

The President's Role

In the United Kingdom, the monarch (king or queen) is the Head of State, but is really the figurehead of the country. For example, Queen Elizabeth II does not play a political or executive role in the government, and is not in charge of making or passing legislation. Those duties are handled by Parliament. However, the queen does serve a purpose because she is the figurehead toward whom the citizens look for stability and unity.

In the United States, the government structure is somewhat similar but also rather different. Like in the United Kingdom, the lawmaking body is separate from the Head of State—it is Congress that creates new legislation, not the president. However, the president does sign off on it. This means that there is a system of **checks and balances** that divides the power among the executive, legislative, and the judicial branches of the U.S. government.

Unlike the monarch in the United Kingdom, the president actually has specifically defined roles as the head of the United States. Some are actually defined in the U.S. Constitution.

Barack Obama gave Bill Clinton the Presidential Medal of Freedom in 2013.

A couple of other duties are also part of the president's role, though they are not defined in the country's Constitution.

Chief of State

The role of chief of state establishes the president as the head of government in the United States. It also establishes the president as the symbol of the people. This is a largely ceremonial but very visible role. Some of the duties a president might perform as chief of state include greeting visitors to the White House, giving speeches to the public, and awarding medals to prominent citizens.

One of the president's responsibilities is appointing the head of the CIA.

Chief Executive

The role of chief executive gives the president executive powers, both on domestic issues and issues of foreign affairs. However, even though the president is officially the chief executive, as set out in the Constitution, their powers are limited by the system of checks and balances. As the representative for just one branch of a three-branched government system, the president does not have supreme power over the nation.

Some of the duties fulfilled by the president as chief executive include appointing the heads of the Central Intelligence Agency (CIA) and the Federal Bureau of Investigation (FBI), and holding cabinet meetings.

Chief Administrator

The role of chief administrator designates the president as the head of the executive branch of government, which means that all of the 2.7 million people who work in that branch of the government technically report to the president. Obviously, there are many levels of management between the president and the lowest-level employees in the executive branch. However, if someone traced the organizational chart all the way from the bottom of the executive branch, the president would be at the top as the chief administrator.

Chief Diplomat

The role of chief diplomat establishes the president as the main creator of foreign policy. The president's foreign policy is followed domestically and abroad by U.S. diplomats and ambassadors. The role also sets up the president as main spokesperson for the United States to foreign countries, though diplomats and ambassadors are spokespersons, too.

President Trump met with German Chancellor Angela Merkel shortly after he took office.

Some of the duties performed by the president as chief diplomat include communicating with foreign leaders, traveling to foreign countries to meet with their leaders, and welcoming foreign leaders to the White House. During the Cold War era, the president's role as chief diplomat was particularly important, because tensions between the United States and Russia could have resulted in nuclear war. Diplomacy has continued to be important as tensions with the Middle East have risen over the past several years.

Commander in Chief

The role of commander in chief puts the president in charge of the U.S. military, including the Army, Navy, Air Force, Marines, and Coast Guard. This role is much like their role as chief administrator, in that members of the armed forces report to the president—even though there are many levels of management in between. Duties performed by the president in the role of commander in chief include determining where U.S. troops will be sent and how weapons will be used, deciding whether to attack foreign cities during wartime, and ordering the National Guard to be deployed to states that may be in crisis.

Since the passage of the Armed Forces Reserve Act in 1952, there have been at least 12 instances in which the president had to deploy the National Guard. For example, the National Guard was called in several times to soothe tensions that erupted during the civil rights era, when schools were being desegregated and racial integration was taking place. The National Guard was sent out for the Alabama civil rights march led by Martin Luther King, Jr. from Selma to Montgomery, and for riots following Martin Luther King, Jr.'s assassination, too. Later, the National Guard was deployed for riots after the Rodney King verdict was delivered in Los Angeles in 1992.

Chief Legislator

The role of chief legislator makes up a large part of the president's duties. This role establishes the president as the person who shapes public policy. This means the president can suggest legislation they feel is needed. That does not mean the legislation will actually become law, though. Officially, Congress is the branch of government that proposes new legislation, and bills go through a long process in Congress before they eventually come to the president's desk to be signed into law. The president works with Congress to suggest potential legislation that they feel is appropriate. The duties of the president in this role include making speeches to Congress about legislation the president is in favor of or would like to see **vetoed**, as well as signing bills that have been passed by Congress.

Party Chief

The president is also the head of the political party they represent. This role is not defined in the Constitution. As the party chief, the president has duties such as nominating party members to serve in the presidential cabinet and campaigning for senators and members of the House of Representatives.

Article II, Section 2, of the Constitution gives the president the right to select a cabinet. It states, "[The president] shall nominate, and by and with the Advice and Consent of the Senate, shall appoint Ambassadors, other public Ministers and Consuls, Judges of the supreme Court, and all other Officers of the United States, whose Appointments are not herein otherwise provided for, and which shall be established by Law: but the Congress may by Law vest the Appointment of such inferior Officers, as they think proper." In other words, the president can nominate members to their cabinet, but the Senate must approve them.

The president works with the House of Representatives and the Senate on new legislation.

The cabinet is designed to be filled with individuals who can advise the president on various issues of national importance. For example, President Donald Trump's cabinet consists of 24 members, including the vice president, secretary of state, attorney general, and secretary of homeland security.

Chief Citizen

The role of chief citizen is largely symbolic. It establishes that the president is the representative of all U.S. citizens. In this role, the president is expected to work for the common interests of all U.S. citizens. This role is not defined in the Constitution, but it is an obvious and very important role for the president.

CONTROVERSIAL CABINET CHOICES

Several of President Trump's proposed cabinet members raised eyebrows, as many people did not feel they were qualified to serve as advisors to the president in such a capacity. For example, Administrator of the Environmental Protection Agency, Scott Pruitt, was contested because he has questioned whether climate change is really an issue and has suggested publicly that there is no scientific evidence proving climate change (an assertion with which scientists strongly disagree). Attorney General Jeff Sessions was a hotly argued nominee because of his reputation for not being supportive of civil rights or disability rights. Secretary of Education Betsy DeVos was also loudly contested because she previously had no experience in the public school system—the cornerstone of education in the United States. Sessions and Pruitt were both narrowly confirmed by the Senate, and DeVos's confirmation was so narrow that, for the first time in history, the vice president had to break a tie vote for a cabinet nominee.

It is worth noting that the Senate nearly always confirms cabinet nominees. In fact, only nine times in history has the Senate rejected a cabinet nominee. Four of these rejections occurred in President John Tyler's cabinet, and most of the rest happened before the 1930s. However, two rejections have occurred in the past 60 years. President Dwight D. Eisenhower's nominee for Secretary of Commerce, Lewis Strauss, was rejected as was President George H.W. Bush's nominee for secretary of defense: John Tower.

Protestors demonstrated over what they felt were poor cabinet choices.

Attorney General Jeff Sessions was a highly unpopular cabinet appointment.

The president's duties are wide and varied, and some extend even beyond these eight official roles. Needless to say, it is a job with a lot of responsibility. President Trump famously stated that he was surprised by how much work being president is, and that it is much harder than his previous job as a businessman.

However, it is a job with much prestige and honor. And for every person who says, "You couldn't pay me enough to take on that job," there is another person who dreams of someday holding that office.

HOW WELL DO YOU
UNDERSTAND
AMERICAN DEMOCRACY?

The president of the United States has more duties and influence than the reigning monarch in the United Kingdom. What do you think are the pros and cons of the U.S. government's structure compared with the British government's structure?

CHAPTER 4

The President and Congress

The executive and legislative branches of government make up two of the three parts of the United States government structure. The president heads the executive branch, and the legislative branch is made up of the two chambers of Congress: the Senate and the House of Representatives. Together, they make laws that are then upheld by the third branch: the judicial branch. At least in theory, the judicial branch can rule against laws it finds **unconstitutional**. Together, the three branches have an elaborate system of checks and balances that help maintain the stability of the nation.

What Congress Does

If the president has ideas about legislation that should be passed, they can suggest that Congress consider introducing a bill covering that legislation. To be introduced in Congress, a bill must have at least one sponsor, though it can (and often does) have multiple co-sponsors. The president can support the bill publicly, but the president cannot officially introduce or sponsor the bill. The annual federal budget is one bill that is introduced at the president's request, though the president may request that other bills be introduced. Technically, anyone can write a bill, but only a member of Congress can officially introduce and sponsor that bill. Once a bill is introduced, the long process of guiding it through both chambers of Congress begins.

The bill is first considered in an appropriate subcommittee, which will read and amend it as needed. The subcommittee will listen to the testimony of experts, **advocates**, and opponents about the strengths and flaws of the bill. There are 104 subcommittees in the House of Representatives and 70 subcommittees in the Senate. The bill will be placed with the appropriate subcommittee.

If the subcommittee rejects the bill, then the bill in its current form never makes it any farther. It can, however, be reintroduced at a later time with changes. If the subcommittee accepts the bill, it moves to the appropriate committee. There are 23 committees in the House of Representatives and 17 in the Senate.

The process in the committee is much the same as in the subcommittee. The bill is read, then reviewed by experts, advocates, opponents, and the committee as a whole, amended as needed, and either rejected or approved. If it is rejected, it goes no farther in its current form. If it is approved, the bill is then reported to the floor of the chamber of Congress in which it was introduced (the House or Senate). The majority party leadership in the particular chamber will put the bill on the calendar for consideration or will put it on hold if it is not a particularly pressing matter.

Congress meets at the United States Capitol in Washington, D.C.

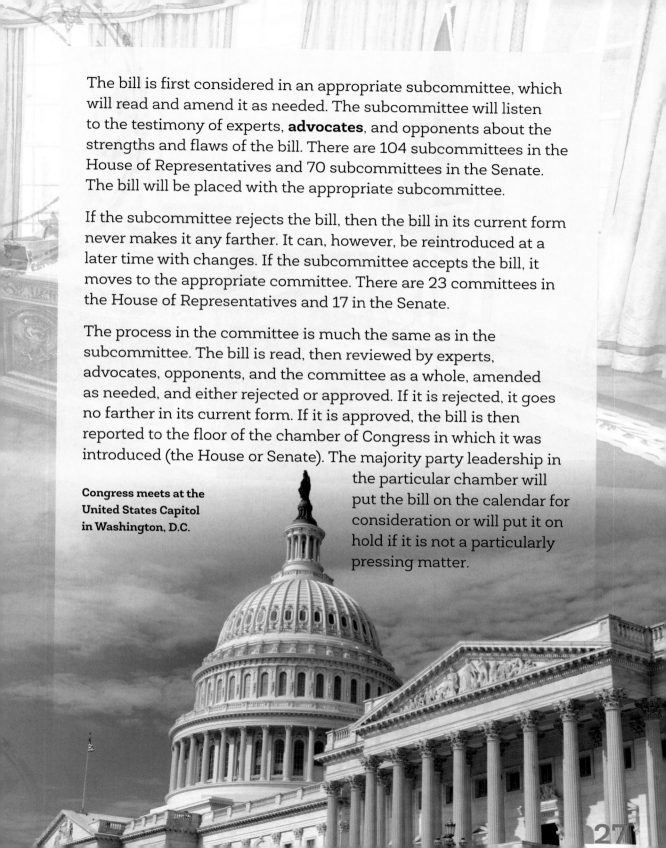

When the bill is brought to the floor, the process depends a bit on whether it was introduced in the House or the Senate. In the House, the debate process is very strict: members of the House may only debate the bill for a couple of minutes, and there are limits to the number and types of amendments that can be made to the bill.

In the Senate, there is more flexibility. Debate is unlimited, and any amendments can be introduced. Senators can also address issues not immediately relevant to the bill during their debate, which gives them an opportunity to filibuster if they wish.

STALLING THE DEBATE

Filibustering is essentially a stalling tactic. A senator who wants to hold the floor so that a bill cannot be moved to a vote can simply keep talking about whatever they want. Until the senator gives up the floor, no vote on the bill can be held.

The longest filibuster in history so far was by South Carolina senator Strom Thurmond, who spoke for 24 hours and 18 minutes in an attempt to block a vote on the Civil Rights Act of 1957, which he opposed. Thurmond spent his time talking about the bill—but also reciting the Declaration of Independence, the Bill of Rights, other historical documents, and the farewell address of President George Washington. The rules of a filibuster say nothing about the senator's speech remaining on the topic of the bill—as long as they keep talking and do not give up the floor, the filibuster continues.

A filibuster can be broken, though. A super majority of 60 senators can use cloture, which is a procedure that ends the filibuster and forces a vote on the bill.

Once all discussion is finished, the bill is voted on. If it is passed in the chamber of Congress in which it was introduced, it then moves to the other chamber and starts the process all over again there.

Rarely do bills pass both chambers with the same wording. The American Health Care Act (AHCA)/Better Care Reconciliation Act (BCRA), which made its way through the chambers of Congress in 2017, is a prime example. The House passed the AHCA, despite much controversy over its contents. The Senate then went to work crafting their own health care bill, which would supposedly address and amend the unpopular parts of the AHCA. The Senate introduced their bill as the BCRA, and it was indeed not the same as the AHCA (though many argued that it was actually worse in terms of threatening the health care of millions of Americans).

Although the AHCA did not pass Congress, the Trump administration has not given up on repealing the Affordable Care Act and will likely propose another alternative.

HOW WELL DO YOU UNDERSTAND AMERICAN DEMOCRACY?

From 1992 to 2012, senators filibustered 942 times. Republicans held the filibuster in 591 of these cases, and Democrats in 352. Why do you think the numbers of filibusters are so uneven between parties? And how do you feel about filibustering being allowed in the Senate? What are the pros and cons to introducing it in the House? Or to outlawing it in both chambers?

The American Health Care Act

What Happens When a Bill Passes Congress?

Once a bill has passed in both chambers, it cannot go to the president for signature with two different versions. So, the bills from the House and Senate go to a Conference Committee that roughly blends together both bills into one final bill. That final bill is then presented to the Speaker of the House and the President of the Senate for their signatures. After those two officers sign off on a bill, it goes to the president for their signature. At that point, the president has a few options:

- The president can sign the bill into law.

- The president can veto the bill.

- The president can take no action, in which case the bill will become law by default in ten days if Congress is still in session.

- The president can take no action, in which case the bill will die if Congress adjourns before the 10-day waiting period is up. This is a pocket veto.

This cartoon shows a veto made by President Chester Arthur in 1882.

Andrew Johnson holds the dubious title of having the most presidential vetoes ever overridden by Congress.

The President's Veto

If the president uses a pocket veto, then the bill dies. Congress is not allowed to override a pocket veto. If Congress still wants the legislation to pass, it must start over with a brand-new bill. If the president vetoes the bill in the traditional way, Congress has the opportunity to override the veto if it wishes. Overriding the veto requires a two-thirds majority vote in each chamber of Congress. Up until the end of President Barack Obama's presidency, Congress had overridden only 111 presidential vetoes. The first time Congress used this power successfully was in overriding a presidential veto by President John Tyler in 1845. The president with the most so far was Andrew Johnson, who had 15 vetoes overridden by Congress.

CHAPTER 5

Presidential Power

The president is a unique position in that, on the surface, it looks very powerful. But in reality, there are a lot of checks and balances on a president's power. During election years, presidential candidates make a lot of promises about what they will do. However, sometimes, the things they promise are not really things they have much power over. So, exactly what powers does a president have?

Power to Make Treaties

According to Article II, Section 2, of the Constitution, "[The President] shall have Power, by and with the Advice and Consent of the Senate, to make **Treaties**, provided two thirds of the Senators present concur." This means that the president has the power to make treaties with other countries, but doing so requires a two-thirds majority vote from the Senate. This is an important presidential power, but not a complete one.

Power over the Military

Article II, Section 2, of the Constitution also states, "The President shall be Commander in Chief of the Army and Navy of the United States, and of the Militia of the several States, when called into the actual Service of the United States." The president can order military operations, which the military will generally carry out as long as they are legal and achievable. Technically, under constitutional law, the president cannot declare war.

Congress must declare war. However, the president can order attacks, missile strikes, operations, and so on, that would commonly occur in war or as part of war-like activities.

This is another example of the separation of power and system of checks and balances the Framers of the Constitution deliberately wrote in. While the president is indeed in charge of the military, they do not have complete power.

Power to Pardon

Article II, Section 2, of the Constitution also gives the president "Power to grant Reprieves and Pardons for Offenses against the United States, except in Cases of Impeachment." In other words, the president can **pardon** a prisoner.

Although this might seem to be a minor power, it is not taken for granted by presidents, who have issued approximately 20,000 pardons and **commutations** in the twentieth century alone. President Bill Clinton, for example, pardoned, commuted, or **rescinded** 459 convictions—one of which was his brother, who was in prison on drug charges. President Obama pardoned or commuted 1,715 convictions. One of the most controversial was his decision to pardon Chelsea Manning, who had been sentenced to 35 years in prison for leaking classified documents to **WikiLeaks**.

Protestors demonstrated in support of Chelsea Manning, whom President Obama later pardoned.

Power to Influence the Makeup of Congress

A presidential administration achieves more when Congress is held by the president's political party. For example, many people think that Barack Obama would have accomplished more as president if the Republican Congress had not opposed many of his ideas. People who disagree with President Trump's decisions and policies are hoping that the next general election will allow Democrats to hold Congress. Democrats could then oppose the president's actions when they disagree with him.

The president does have some power when it comes to influencing the makeup of Congress. First, presidents are allowed to publicly express support for any candidate for the House or Senate—and naturally, a president will back a candidate from their own party. Having presidential backing is generally considered a positive for a candidate—a guarantee of more votes.

The Constitution also gives the president the power to fill Senate vacancies. Article II, Section 2, states "The President shall have Power to fill up all Vacancies that may happen during the Recess of the Senate, by granting Commissions which shall expire at the End of their next Session." In theory, then, the president could fill Senate vacancies with senators from their own political party.

While the president does not appoint members of Congress, they have some influence over who is elected.

However, Congress has the option to reject such an appointment so, again, this is not a complete power on the part of the president.

Power to Nominate Supreme Court Justices

The president also has the power to nominate Supreme Court justices. This might seem to be a minor power, but it is actually incredibly important. The Supreme Court sets legal **precedent** for the entire nation. If a president wants to see legislation enacted in a particular manner, it is in the president's best interest to balance the Supreme Court toward their own agenda.

Nominating Supreme Court justices is a powerful part of the president's job.

Currently, the Supreme Court has eight justices. Four tend to be **liberal**, and four tend to be **conservative**. However, in recent years, the Supreme Court has ruled on a lot of liberal-leaning legislation, such as marriage equality (allowing same-sex couples the right to marry), women's rights issues, disability rights issues, and so on. While it is unwise to say that all liberals support these issues and no conservatives support them, these issues generally tend to be important to liberal Americans.

President Obama tended to support this liberal legislation. However, President Trump is a conservative president, and conservative Americans hope to see some of this liberal legislation change. Conservatives often do not support marriage equality, pro-choice legislation, and other similarly liberal agendas. Since much of this involves interpreting constitutional law, the place to make the changes conservatives hope to see is in the Supreme Court. In theory, a conservative-leaning Supreme Court could overturn recent legislation supporting marriage equality, and some hope that a conservative-leaning Supreme Court would rule favorably on Donald Trump's proposed stricter immigration policies. Some even hope to eventually see the landmark *Row v. Wade* legislation overturned someday, even though it has been in place for decades. So that might be difficult to change, even for a conservative Supreme Court.

The White House lit up in rainbow colors to show its support after the Supreme Court ruled in favor of marriage equality.

SUPREME COURT BALANCE

In 2016, there was an opening on the Supreme Court because conservative Justice Antonin Scalia passed away. President Barack Obama tried to fill his seat with a moderate, Merrick Garland, who would have kept the court in balance. However, the Republican Senate refused to confirm the nomination, so the seat remained open.

Supreme Court Justice Antonin Scalia passed away in 2016, leaving the conservative side of the bench a bit lighter.

In 2017, President Trump nominated Judge Neil Gorsuch, and the Senate confirmed his choice. Some fear this will tip the balance to the conservative side, and could ultimately result in liberal legislation being overturned.

One of the strongly liberal members of the Supreme Court, Justice Ruth Bader Ginsburg, is more than 80 years old, and there are questions about whether she will retire. If Justice Ginsburg steps down for any reason and opens a vacancy on the Supreme Court, it is yet another opportunity for a conservative presidential administration to appoint a justice who will uphold conservative legislation and likely vote against liberal legislation. The hope of liberal citizens is that Justice Ginsburg will remain in the court until the Senate turns over to Democratic power. That way, a Republican Senate will not be able to confirm a conservative justice to take her place.

CHAPTER 6
Controversy and Strife

While the presidency is an esteemed and respected office, not every president has been a model of **decorum**. In fact, there has been some level of strife and controversy in probably every presidency. Even the much-loved President John F. Kennedy had his failings. Some presidents, however, have been more controversial than others and some presidencies have been ended by tragedy, which changed history in a moment.

Assassinations

There have been more than 30 assassination attempts on presidents, former presidents, and presidents-elect. However, only four sitting presidents have actually been assassinated: Abraham Lincoln, James Garfield, William McKinley, and John F. Kennedy.

John Wilkes Booth, a **Confederate** sympathizer, shot President Abraham Lincoln in 1865.

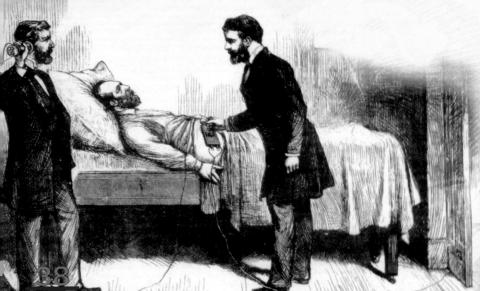

James Garfield was one of the four presidents who have been assassinated while in office.

Booth was strongly opposed to ending slavery, and Lincoln had started the process of ending slavery when he signed the Emancipation Proclamation in 1863. Booth shot President Lincoln in the back of the head, and Lincoln died the next morning.

In 1881, after only four months in office, President James Garfield was shot by Charles Guiteau. Guiteau was reportedly frustrated that Garfield had not named him ambassador to France. Garfield actually did not die immediately from the gunshot wounds. Instead, he died nearly three months later from infections related to the wounds.

THE LUCKY SURVIVORS

Two other sitting presidents survived shootings: Theodore Roosevelt and Ronald Reagan. Many other presidents survived assassination attempts but were not actually shot. Roosevelt and Reagan, however, were shot and survived.

In Milwaukee in 1912, John F. Schrank shot President Theodore Roosevelt in the chest, just before the president was scheduled to deliver a speech. Amazingly, President Roosevelt refused to go directly to the hospital. Instead, he insisted on delivering his 90-minute speech as planned. He reportedly told the crowd that it would take more than a bullet to kill a "bull moose." Oddly enough, the 50 pages of notes Roosevelt had prepared for his speech likely saved his life. Roosevelt had the thick set of papers in his jacket, and the bullet tore through them and slowed down before entering his chest. The bullet stayed in Roosevelt's body up until his death in 1919.

In 1981, John Hinckley Jr. shot President Ronald Reagan. Hinckley reportedly said he was motivated to kill President Reagan in an effort to impress actress Jodie Foster. However, Jodie Foster had no knowledge of this plan (and nothing against President Reagan), and Hinckley was found to be insane.

President William McKinley's 1901 assassination was also politically motivated. He was shot by an **anarchist** named Leon Czolgosz, though it is not entirely clear what Czolgosz's specific motivation was, other than a general dislike for organized government. Czolgosz refused to speak to anyone—even his defense attorney—about the crime and his motivations.

In 1963, Lee Harvey Oswald assassinated President John F. Kennedy. Oswald's motive for shooting the president is unknown, in part because Oswald himself was assassinated (by man named Jack Ruby) just two days after he killed the president. There have long been rumors that Kennedy's assassination was part of a large conspiracy, but no one knows for sure.

This image of President John F. Kennedy in the motorcade in Dallas, Texas, was taken just before he was assassinated.

Impeachments

Only the House of Representatives can start impeachment proceedings against a president. However, it is the Senate that hears the trial and rules on the impeachment. The Senate has to vote by a two-thirds majority to impeach a president. The House has so far only impeached two presidents: Andrew Johnson and Bill Clinton. However, the Senate acquitted both men and neither faced criminal charges. It is widely believed that President Richard Nixon was impeached, but that is untrue. When news of his involvement in a cover-up of the Watergate scandal became public knowledge, Nixon resigned before he could be impeached.

Richard Nixon faced impeachment, but resigned before it could happen.

Johnson had 11 articles of impeachment brought against him for high crimes and wrongdoings, as set out in Article II of the Constitution. Vice President Johnson had come to be president when Abraham Lincoln was assassinated. This was during the **Reconstruction Era** after the Civil War. Johnson and Congress clashed in their policies. Congress felt that Johnson's plan was far too lenient on the South and former slaveholders.

Johnson suspended and replaced Secretary of War Edwin Stanton, who was important to Congress's Reconstruction efforts. This violated the newly passed **Tenure of Office Act**, which led to the House calling for Johnson's impeachment. There were other similar charges brought against Johnson, but his violation of the Tenure of Office Act was the trigger for his impeachment proceedings.

The Senate narrowly acquitted Johnson on the impeachment charges, and he was able to complete his term in office. However, he was not reelected when his term ended.

President Bill Clinton also had articles of impeachment brought against him by the House, in the name of perjury and obstruction of justice. As with Johnson, Clinton had a number of issues that led up to his impeachment proceedings. But the charges were a result of Clinton admitting he had lied to the grand jury when questioned about an affair he had with a White House intern. The Senate voted to acquit Clinton of impeachment charges, and he was allowed to finish his second term in office.

In 2017, the House was considering bringing articles of impeachment against President Trump based on numerous allegations of his wrongdoings in office, such as his rumored involvement in the alleged Russian hacking of the 2016 election. In October of that year, House Representative Al Green brought articles of impeachment against President Trump on the grounds that he incited bigotry and hatred. Green did not include accusations of specific crimes, but argued that a president does not have to commit a crime to warrant impeachment. Congress voted against impeachment, although 58 Democracts supported the measure. It is possible for the House to bring articles of impeachment against a President more than once.

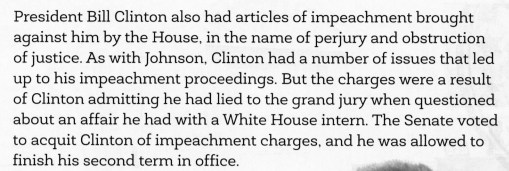

President Bill Clinton faced impeachment, but was acquitted.

The President's Future

President Trump has declared that he will "Make America Great Again," but public opinion on that idea is mixed. Some people really do believe he has the vision to guide the country through troubled times and continue to build its reputation as a world superpower. Others feel that he is destroying the very principles on which the United States was founded—as a home and a safe place for all who wish to be citizens—and is destroying the relationships that past presidents have carefully built with other foreign nations.

Despite being sometimes plagued by controversy, scandal, and misfortune, the office of the presidency remains the highest and most esteemed office in the U.S. government system. The three-branched system of government remains intact, and the system of checks and balances that the Framers so carefully set forth in the Constitution continue to define the office of the presidency. In the future, there is no doubt that the roles and responsibilities of the president will likely shift and transform in small ways. Presidential duties will no doubt be expanded in some areas, and perhaps restricted in others.

The White House is the home of the president while they are in office.

The President in Action

Chief of state

Chief executive

Chief administrator

Chief diplomat

Commander in chief

Chief legislator

Party chief

Chief citizen

- Making speeches, awarding medals and other prizes, greeting White House visitors

- Holding cabinet meetings, appointing the heads of the FBI and CIA

- The "boss" of all employees of the executive branch

- Communicating with foreign leaders and meeting with foreign leaders, either in their home country or at the White House

- Heading the U.S. armed forces, and deploying National Guard and reserve troops as needed

- Signing bills that have passed Congress into law and working with Congress to shape public policy

- Heading the party that elected them to office, nominating officials to the presidential cabinet, and supporting senators and representatives from the president's party

- Representing the best interests of all U.S. citizens

Glossary

advocates People who recommend or support something publicly.

anarchist A person who supports individual freedom and the absence of official government.

caucuses Meetings at which members of a political party choose among candidates running for office.

checks and balances A system that balances power, ensuring that all power is not left in the hands of one individual or small group.

commutations Reductions to a less severe judicial sentence.

Confederate Someone who fought for or supported the 11 southern states that seceded from the United States in the Civil War era.

conservative Describes one who values traditional systems and is cautious about new innovation.

decorum Good taste and propriety.

electoral college The body of official voters, representing each state, who formally cast the votes for the president of the United States.

figurehead A leader who has no real power.

Framers of the Constitution The delegates who went to the Constitutional Convention and ultimately drafted the Constitution.

indirect vote The voting system used for the office of president in which citizens vote for their candidate but, in reality, are casting a vote for a member of the electoral college, who then officially votes for the candidate in the presidential election.

liberal Describes one who is open to new ideas and innovation and is willing to change traditional systems.

naturalized Earned citizenship to a country.

pardon To forgive the legal consequences for a conviction.

popular vote A simple form of election in which the candidate with the most votes wins.

precedent An action or event that is regarded as an example or guide for future similar circumstances.

ratified Given formal consent to a new law, treaty, contract, or agreement, thus making it valid.

Reconstruction Era The post-Civil War era in which the government attempted to rebuild the United States and help the Confederacy reintegrate into the nation as a whole.

rescinded Revoked or repealed.

Tenure of Office Act A federal law in place from 1867 to 1887 that restricted the president's power of removing an official from office without Senate approval.

treaties Formal, ratified agreements between two or more countries.

unconstitutional Against what is stated in a political constitution.

vetoed Rejected.

WikiLeaks An organization that publishes classified information gained from anonymous sources.

For More Information

Books

Matuz, Roger. *The Presidents Fact Book: The Achievements, Campaigns, Events, Triumphs, and Legacies of Every President*. New York, NY: Black Dog & Leventhal, 2016.

O'Brien, Cormac. *Secret Lives of the U.S. Presidents: Strange Stories and Shocking Trivia from Inside the White House*. Philadelphia, PA: Quirk Books, 2017.

Ricks, Ingrid (ed.). *Dear Mr. President: Teen Voices from Across the Country*. Ingrid Ricks, 2017.

Smith, Carter. *Presidents: Every Question Answered*. San Diego, CA: Thunder Bay Press, 2017.

Websites

This website contains explanations about how various aspects of U.S. government function:
www.kids.usa.gov/teens/goverment/index.shtml

The Library of Congress website is searchable and full of great information about U.S. history and government:
www.loc.gov

The National Archives is another fantastic resource for researching historical documents and facts:
www.archives.gov

National Geographic's education page has links to many resources about U.S. history and government:
www.nationalgeographic.org/education

Publisher's note to educators and parents: Our editors have carefully reviewed these websites to ensure that they are suitable for students. Many websites change frequently, however, and we cannot guarantee that a site's future contents will continue to meet our high standards of quality and educational value. Be advised that students should be closely supervised whenever they access the Internet.

Index